Touching the
Divine

Touching the Divine

How to Make Your Daily Life a Conversation with God

Featuring Two Classics of Contemplative Life *(The Cloud of Unknowing* and *The Practice of the Presence of God)* and the Centering Prayer That Emerged from Them

EDITED AND INTERPRETED BY GAY HENDRICKS AND JAMES TWYMAN

THE TRANSFORMATIONAL BOOK CIRCLE

Ojai, California

Published by: The Transformational Book Circle, 402 W. Ojai Ave., Ojai, CA 93023 • 866-288-4469 (customer service) • 866-300-4386 (orders) • www.transformationalbookcircle.com • info@transformationalbookcircle.com

Editorial supervision: Jill Kramer • *Design:* Tricia Breidenthal

ISBN 13: 978-1-4019-1025-9
ISBN 10: 1-4019-1025-4

08 07 06 05   4 3 2 1
1st printing, October 2005

Printed in the United States of America

CONTENTS

INTRODUCTION

Y ou are holding in your hands a most precious resource for personal and spiritual transformation. The material in this volume delivers a message that has touched millions of lives since it first came to light hundreds of years ago. Both the anonymous author of *The Cloud of Unknowing* and the monk known as Brother Lawrence are concerned with a single subject of great importance for anyone on a spiritual path: how to carry on an intimate conversation with God in every moment. The goal is union with God, but the union these authors address is of a special sort. They're not interested in the concept of union, but in the actual feeling of unity you can experience in your body. This in itself would be reason to read these books, but there is more . . . a great deal more.

First, these are works that teach practical tools of transcendence. The most famous tool is the Centering Prayer, used by millions of seekers over the past several hundred years. This prayer is carefully described later in the book. The spoken-word CD that accompanies this book will give you a thorough grounding in this powerful technique.

Ultimately, though, love is the underground river that nourishes the wisdom in this work. The authors are emphatic that their path is love. Their point is that the intellect is not only a poor conductor of God's energy, it is also the major barrier or cloud of illusion that keeps the sincere seeker from resonance and merger with the being of God.

Both authors come from the Christian monastic tradition; however, the message they bring speaks clearly to Buddhists, Muslims, and seekers from other spiritual paths. These wise men know that an inner monk lives inside all of us, no matter how worldly we may be. They know the hunger for union with God that lives within every sincere spiritual seeker.

The Cloud of Unknowing is the better known of the two books that comprise this volume. However, very little is known of the 14th-century monk who wrote it. When you read his words and tune in to his distinctive voice, you may wish, as many others have, that we knew more about him.

Gay: That was my feeling when I first encountered the man who wrote <ins>The Cloud of Unknowing</ins>. Once I got through the thorny thickets of the language it was written in, I found something refreshingly clear and to-the-point about the book. Often the author was blunt and anything but humble. For a person who lived in a time of rigid hierarchy, he wrote in a conversational way that was directed not at his fellow monks, but to human beings everywhere.

What gave him this confidence to speak across the centuries to the entire community of seekers? I believe it was his personal experience and the sincerity of his intent. As I immersed myself in his world, I came to realize that the only way to appreciate it fully was to match the author's sincere intention for union with God with as much of my own sincerity as I could muster. When I did so, I was rewarded by much deeper and richer experiences.

If you're sincere in your intention to feel close to divinity in every moment, you're surely to be rewarded with many such rich experiences as you walk through the world of *The Cloud of Unknowing*.

Now, for the second jewel of the contemplative literature we explore in this volume. Originally called *The Practice of the Presence of God*, Brother Lawrence's little book has inspired generations of contemplatives.

James: When his book came into my hands many years ago, I was a young seminary student on fire with religious passion, and in great turmoil about the world inside me and outside me. I had gloriously lofty ideals, but I also suffered terrible challenges putting those ideals into living reality in my life. Then came Brother Lawrence. His gentle, clear wisdom was

like a breath of fresh air through my life. I found my inner conflicts melting, and my abilities to practice my faith growing stronger each time I read this little miracle of a book.

I cannot think of a greater gift you can give yourself than to spend a minute or two now and then with the eternal wisdom of Brother Lawrence. He's been my spiritual brother and teacher for decades now, and each year his words mean more to me than ever before.

Who Was Brother Lawrence?

The man known as Brother Lawrence was born Nicholas Herman in the early 1600s in Lorraine, a Duchy of France. Little is known about his birth, because the records were destroyed in a fire at his parish church during the Thirty Years War (in which young Nicholas fought as a soldier). It was during his war years that he suffered a nearly fatal injury that left him crippled and in pain throughout his life. From what we know of him,

Brother Lawrence was drawn to the spiritual life from an early age. In his youth he was tutored by a priest named Lawrence, in honor of whom the young Nicholas Herman likely took his monastic name.

Before entering life as a monk, Brother Lawrence spent a period of time living in the wilderness, inspired by the desert fathers of the beginnings of Christian history. He was a butler or household servant for a period of time, and by his own account he did not distinguish himself in this occupation. He said he "was clumsy and broke everything."

When he entered the monastery at midlife, he began as the cook for the community of monks. Later, he became employed in the monastery's sandal-repair shop. None of these humble occupations can account for the moving eloquence with which he expresses himself in the letters that are at the heart of his book.

What Can He Teach Us Today?

Brother Lawrence's path is a simple one, and we believe that this simplicity is what resonates so deeply with people of our busy time. He tells us, clearly and gently, how to walk the spiritual path in a pure and straightforward way. The trials and tribulations he faces are the same ones we encounter today, and his attitude toward those stumbling blocks can teach us much about how to deal with them in our own time of great challenge.

In these pages you'll discover a gentleman in the truest sense of the word (a gentle man), and one whose spirit sings with great joy. He attracted little fame and certainly no fortune during his sojourn on Earth. It was only after his death that a few of his letters were collected. Joseph de Beaufort, counsel to the Paris archbishop, first published the letters in a small pamphlet. The following year, in a publication that he titled "The Practice of the Presence of God," de Beaufort included the four conversations he had with Brother Lawrence.

Brother Lawrence shows us how to walk and talk with God in a new yet very ancient tongue: the language of the heart. His gentle clarity nourishes us as well today as when his words first sprang forth from the heart of this joyous monk. When Brother Lawrence died in 1691, he had practiced God's presence for more than 40 years.

In Summary

These simple instructions pervade the work we've drawn on here:

- Approach God through the heart, not the mind.

- Approach God with sincerity of intent.

- When you notice yourself wandering from your intent to know God in every moment, do not judge or criticize yourself—simply return to your heart's desire to touch the Divine.

Those are the instructions, and this is the promise: Do these simple things and you will experience many holy moments of connection with the Infinite.

May you be as deeply touched as we have been by Brother Lawrence and the anonymous monk who wrote *The Cloud of Unknowing.*

— **Gay Hendricks and James Twyman**

Chapter One

FOUR CONVERSATIONS
WITH A MASTER OF
CONTEMPLATION

Introducing the Conversations

What comes down through history from Brother Lawrence is due to the efforts of Joseph de Beaufort, who sought out the monk and recorded his conversations in a notebook. When Joseph de Beaufort first had these conversations with Brother Lawrence, the gentle monk was already in his late 50s and in charge of the monastery's sandal-repair shop. Sandal repair was an important part of service in a monastery, and de Beaufort noted that Brother Lawrence's shop handled more than 100 pairs of sandals.

When de Beaufort, worldly friend of the rich and famous, first met Brother Lawrence, he found the monk "rough in appearance" but also "gentle in grace." We don't know whether these conversations took place in the sandal shop or strolling the monastery's grounds or over a glass of the monastery's best wine. All we now have are the words themselves and the aura of radiance that you, the sensitive reader, can feel around you. Once you spend time with those words and resonate with them, you may feel as we do that little else needs to be added. Accordingly, we've done relatively little editing beyond modernizing some of the language and clarifying a few obscure meanings.

The First Conversation

The first time I saw Brother Lawrence was on the 3rd of August, 1666. He told me that God had done him a

special favor in converting him at the age of 18. During that winter he saw a tree stripped of its leaves and realized that within a little time the leaves would be renewed, and after that, the flowers and fruit would appear. Brother Lawrence received a high view of the providence and power of God, which has never since left his soul. This view had perfectly set him free from the world and kindled in him such a love for God that he could not tell whether it had increased in the 40 years that he had lived since.

Brother Lawrence said he had been a servant to M. Fieubert, the treasurer, and that as a footman he was a great, awkward fellow who broke everything. He decided to enter a monastery thinking that he would there be punished for his awkwardness and the faults he would commit, so he would sacrifice to God his life with its pleasures. Brother Lawrence said that God had disappointed him because he met with nothing but satisfaction in that state (instead of being punished).

Brother Lawrence said that we should engage God in a continual conversation. He said that this was the best way to practice God's presence. He said that it was a shameful thing to quit His conversation to think of trifles and fooleries. We should feed and nourish our soul with high notions of God, which would yield us great joy in being devoted to Him.

Brother Lawrence said that we ought to quicken and give life to our faith. It was lamentable that we had so little. Instead of taking faith for the rule of their conduct, men amused themselves with trivial devotions that changed daily.

He said:

- Faith was sufficient to bring us to a high degree of perfection.

- We ought to give ourselves to God both in things temporal and spiritual, and seek our satisfaction only in the fulfilling of His will. Whether God led us by suffering or by consolation, all would be equal to a soul truly resigned.

- We need fidelity in those disruptions in the ebb and flow of prayer when God tries our love to Him. This was the time for a complete act of resignation, whereof one act alone could greatly promote our spiritual advancement.

Brother Lawrence said that as far as the miseries and sins he heard of daily in the world, he was so far from wondering at them, that on the contrary, he was surprised there were not more, considering the malice that sinners were capable of. For his part, he prayed for them; but knowing that God could remedy the mischief they did when He pleased, he gave himself no further trouble.

Brother Lawrence said that to arrive at such resignation as God requires, we should carefully watch over all the passions that mingle in spiritual as well as temporal things. God would give light concerning those passions to those who truly desire to serve Him.

At the end of this first conversation, Brother Lawrence said that if my purpose for the visit was to sincerely discuss how to serve God, I might come to him as often as

I pleased, and without any fear of being troublesome. If this was not the case, then I ought visit him no more.

The Second Conversation

Brother Lawrence told me that he had always been governed by love and not selfishness. Since he resolved to make the love of God the end of all his actions, he had found reasons to be well satisfied with his method. He was pleased when he could take up a straw from the ground for the love of God, seeking Him only, and nothing else, not even His gifts.

He said he had been long troubled in mind from a certain belief that he should be damned. All the men in the world could not have persuaded him to the contrary. This trouble of mind lasted four years, during which time he suffered greatly.

Finally, he reasoned: "I did not engage in a religious life but for the love of God. I have endeavored to act only for Him. Whatever becomes of me, whether I be

lost or saved, I will always continue to act purely for the love of God. I shall know at least that until death I shall have done all that is in me to love Him."

From that time on, Brother Lawrence lived his life in perfect liberty and continual joy. He placed his sins between himself and God and told Him that he did not deserve His favors, yet God still continued to bestow them in abundance.

Brother Lawrence said that in order to form a habit of conversing with God continually and referring all we do to Him, we must, at first, apply to Him with diligence. Then, after a little care, we would find His love inwardly draw us to Him without any difficulty.

He expected after the pleasant days God had given him that he would have his turn of pain and suffering. Yet he was not uneasy about it. Knowing that, since he could do nothing of himself, God would not fail to give him the strength to bear them.

When an occasion of practicing some virtue was offered, he addressed himself to God, saying, "Lord, I cannot do this unless You enable me." Then he received strength more than sufficient. When he had failed in his duty, he only confessed his fault, saying to God, "I shall never do otherwise, if You leave me to myself. It is You who must hinder my failing and mend what is missing." Then, after this, he gave himself no further uneasiness about it.

Brother Lawrence said we ought to act with God in the greatest simplicity, speaking to Him frankly and plainly, and imploring His assistance in our affairs just as they happen. God never failed to grant it, as Brother Lawrence had often experienced.

He said he had been sent recently into Burgundy to buy the provision of wine for the community. This was a very unwelcome task for him because he had no turn for business and because he was lame and could only move around the boat by rolling himself over the casks. Yet he gave himself no uneasiness about it, nor about the purchase of the wine. He said to God that it was His business he was about, and that he afterwards found it very well performed. He mentioned that it had turned out the same way the year before when he was sent to Auvergne.

So, likewise, in his work in the kitchen (to which he

had, at first, a great dislike), having accustomed himself to do everything there for the love of God and asking for His grace to do his work well, he had found everything easy during the 15 years he had worked there. He was well pleased with the post he was now in. Yet, he was as ready to quit that as the former, since he tried to please God by doing little things for the love of Him in any work he did. With him the set times of prayer were no different from other times. He retired to pray according to the directions of his superior, but he did not need such retirement or ask for it because his greatest labor did not divert him from God.

Since he knew his obligation to love God in all things, and as he endeavored to do so, he had no need of a director to advise him, but he greatly needed a confessor to absolve him. He said he was very aware of his faults, but not discouraged by them. He confessed them to God and made no excuses. Then, he peaceably resumed his usual practice of love and adoration.

In his troubled mind, Brother Lawrence had consulted no one. Knowing only by the light of faith that

God was present, he contented himself with directing all his actions to Him. He did everything with a desire to please God and allow what would come of it.

He said that useless thoughts spoil all, and that all mischief began with those thoughts. We ought to reject useless thoughts quickly and return to our communion with God. In the beginning, he had often passed his time appointed for prayer in rejecting wandering thoughts and falling right back into them. He could never regulate his devotion by certain methods, as some do. At first, he had practiced meditation, but after some time, that went off in a manner of which he could give no account.

Brother Lawrence emphasized that all physical and mental disciplines and exercises were useless unless they served to arrive at the union with God by love. He had well considered this. He found that the shortest way to go straight to God was by a continual exercise of love, and doing all things for His sake.

Also, he noted that there was a great difference between acts of the intellect and acts of the will. Acts of the intellect were of comparatively little value. Acts of the will were all-important. Our only business was to love and delight ourselves in God.

He then said that all possible kinds of self-sacrifice, if they were devoid of the love of God, could not efface a single sin. Instead, we ought, without anxiety, to expect the pardon of our sins from the blood of Jesus Christ, endeavoring only to love him with all our heart. He noted that God seemed to have granted the greatest favors to the greatest sinners as more proof of His mercy.

Brother Lawrence said that the greatest pains or pleasures of this world were nothing compared to what he had experienced of both kinds in a spiritual state. As a result, he feared nothing, desiring only one thing of God: that he might not offend Him. He said he carried no guilt, because "when I fail in my duty, I readily acknowledge it, saying I am used to do so. I shall never do otherwise if I am left to myself. If I do not fail, then I immediately give God thanks, acknowledging that it comes from Him."

The Third Conversation

Brother Lawrence told me that the foundation of the spiritual life in him had been a high notion and esteem of God in faith. When he had once well established his faith, he had no other care but to reject every other thought so he might perform all his actions for the love of God. He said that when sometimes he had not thought of God for a good while, he did not disquiet himself. Having acknowledged his wretchedness to God, he simply returned to Him with so much the greater trust.

He said the trust we put in God honors Him and draws down His great grace. It was impossible not only that God should deceive, but that He should long let a soul suffer that is perfectly resigned to Him, and resolved to endure everything for His sake.

Brother Lawrence often experienced the immediate nourishment of Divine Grace. Because of his experience of grace, when he had business to do so, he did not think of it beforehand. When it was time to do it, he found in God, as in a clear mirror, all that was fit for him to do.

When outward business diverted him a little from the thought of God, a fresh remembrance coming from God invested his soul and so inflamed and transported him that it was difficult for him to contain himself. He said he was more united to God in his outward employments than when he left them for devotion in retirement.

Brother Lawrence said that the worst that could happen to him was to lose that sense of God that he had enjoyed so long. Yet the goodness of God assured him that He would not forsake him utterly and that He would give him strength to bear whatever He permitted to happen to him. Brother Lawrence, therefore, said he feared nothing. He had no occasion to consult with anybody about his state. In the past, when he had attempted to do it, he had always come away more perplexed. Since Brother Lawrence was ready to lay down his life for the love of God, he had no apprehension of danger.

He said that perfect relaxation into God was a sure way to heaven, a way in which we always have sufficient light for our conduct. In the beginning of the spiritual life, we ought to be faithful in doing our duty and denying ourselves, and then, after a time, unspeakable pleasures followed. In difficulties we need only turn to Jesus Christ and beg his grace, with which everything became easier.

Brother Lawrence said that many do not advance in Christian progress because they stick in penances and particular exercises, while they neglect the love of God, which is the end. This appeared plainly by their works and was the reason why they see so little solid virtue. He said there needed neither art nor science for going to God, but only a heart resolutely determined to apply itself to nothing but Him and to love Him only.

The Fourth Conversation

Brother Lawrence spoke with great openness of heart concerning his manner of going to God. He told me that all consists in one hearty renunciation of everything that we know does not lead to God. We only need to converse with Him freely and simply. We need only recognize God intimately present with us and address ourselves to

Him every moment. We need to beg His assistance for knowing His will in things doubtful and for rightly performing those things that we plainly see He requires of us, offering them to Him before we do them, and giving God thanks when we have completed them.

In our conversation with God, we should engage in praising, adoring, and loving Him incessantly for His infinite goodness and perfection. Without being discouraged because of our sins, we should pray for His grace with perfect confidence, relying on the infinite merits of our Lord. Brother Lawrence said that God never failed offering us His grace at each action. It never failed except when Brother Lawrence's thoughts had wandered from a sense of God's presence, or he forgot to ask His assistance. He said that God always gave us light in our doubts when we had no other design but to please Him.

Our sanctification did not depend upon changing our works. Instead, it depended on doing those things for God's sake, which we commonly do for our own. He thought it was lamentable to see how many people mistook the means for the end, addicting themselves to certain works that they performed very imperfectly because of their human or selfish regard. The most excellent method he had found for going to God was that of doing our common business without any view of pleasing men, but purely for the love of God.

Brother Lawrence felt that it was a great delusion to think that the times of prayer ought to differ from other times. We are as strictly obliged to adhere to God by action in the time of action, as by prayer in its time. His own prayer was simply a sense of the presence of God, his soul being at that time aware of nothing other than Divine love. When the appointed times of prayer were past, he found no difference, because he still continued with God, praising and thanking Him with all his might. Thus, his life was a continual joy.

Brother Lawrence said we ought, once and for all, to heartily put our whole trust in God, and make a total surrender of ourselves to Him, secure that He would not deceive us. We ought not become weary of doing little things for the love of God, who regards not the greatness of the work, but the love with which it is performed. We should not wonder if, in the beginning, we often failed in our endeavors, but that at last we should gain a habit that will naturally produce its acts in us without our effort and to our great delight.

The whole substance of religion is faith, hope, and charity. In the practice of these, we become united to the will of God. Everything else is indifferent and to be used as a means that we may arrive at our end and then be swallowed up by faith and charity. All things are possible to him who believes. They are less difficult to him who hopes. They are more easy to him who loves, and still more easy to him who perseveres in the practice of these three virtues. The end we ought to propose to ourselves is to become, in this life, the most perfect worshipers of God we can possibly be, and as we hope to be through all eternity.

We must, from time to time, honestly consider and thoroughly examine ourselves. We will, then, realize that we are worthy of great contempt. Brother Lawrence noted that when we directly confront ourselves in this manner, we will understand why we are subject to all kinds of misery and problems. We will realize why we are subject to changes and fluctuations in our health, mental outlook, and dispositions. And we will, indeed, recognize that we deserve all the pain and labor God sends to humble us.

After this, we should not wonder that troubles, temptations, oppositions, and contradictions happen to us from men. We ought, on the contrary, submit ourselves to them and bear them as long as God pleases, as things highly advantageous to us. The greater perfection a soul aspires after, the more dependent it is upon Divine Grace.

Being questioned by one of his own community (to whom he was obliged to respond) as to what means he had attained such an habitual sense of God, Brother Lawrence told him that since first coming to the monastery, he had considered God as the aim and the end of all his thoughts and desires.

In the beginning, he spent the hours appointed for private prayer in thinking of God, so as to convince his mind and impress deeply upon his heart the Divine Existence. He did this by devout sentiments and submission to the lights

Transformational Book Circle™
the book that changed my life

Your Quick Summary And Discussion Guide

TOUCHING THE DIVINE: How To Make Your
Daily Life A Conversation With God

What if a book could change your life?

of faith, rather than by studied reasonings and elaborate meditations. By this short and sure method, he immersed himself in the knowledge and love of God. He resolved to use his utmost endeavor to live in a continual sense of His presence, and, if possible, never to forget Him more.

When he had thus, in prayer, filled his mind with that Infinite Being, he went to his work in the kitchen where he was then cook for the community. There, having first considered the things his job required, and when and how each thing was to be done; he spent all the intervals of his time, both before and after his work, in prayer.

When he began, he said to God with a filial trust, "O my God, since You are with me, and I must now, in obedience to Your commands, apply my mind to these outward things, grant me the grace to continue in Your Presence; and prosper me with Your assistance. Receive all my works, and possess all my affections." As he proceeded in his work, he continued his familiar conversation with his Maker, imploring His grace, and offering Him all his actions.

When he was finished, he examined how he had

performed his duty. If he found well, he returned thanks to God. If not, he asked pardon and, without being discouraged, he set his mind right again. He then continued his exercise of the presence of God as if he had never deviated from it. "Thus," said he, "by rising after my falls, and by frequently renewed acts of faith and love, I have come to a state where it would be as difficult for me not to think of God as it was at first to accustom myself to the habit of thinking of Him."

As Brother Lawrence had found such an advantage in walking in the presence of God, it was natural for him to recommend it earnestly to others. More strikingly, his example was a stronger inducement than any arguments he could propose. His very countenance was edifying with such a sweet and calm devotion appearing that he could not but affect the beholders.

It was observed that even in the busiest times in the kitchen, Brother Lawrence still preserved his recollection and heaven-mindedness. He was never hasty or loitering, but did each thing in its turn with an even, uninterrupted composure and serenity of spirit.

"The time of work," said he, "does not with me differ from the time of prayer. In the noise and clatter of my kitchen, while several persons are at the same time calling for different things, I possess God in as great a serenity as if I were upon my knees at the Blessed Supper."

Chapter Two

FOURTEEN LETTERS OF BROTHER LAWRENCE

Introduction to the Letters

Brother Lawrence's letters were written during the last ten years of his life. He wrote the letters to long-time friends, to a Carmelite sister and another nun at a nearby convent. We don't know for certain, but it's likely that one or both of these friends were from his native village. They may have even been relatives.

The first letter was probably written to the head of one of these convents. The second letter was written to Brother Lawrence's personal spiritual adviser. In some of the letters it's not entirely clear to whom he was writing, and so for those we have addressed them "To my correspondent." In his day it was traditional to substitute the initial M for specific names. We maintain that tradition in this version of Brother Lawrence's letters.

◇◇◇

The First Letter

To a nun:

How I found God's Presence and made it habitual.

You so earnestly desire that I describe the method by which I arrived at that habitual sense of God's presence, which our merciful Lord has been pleased to grant me. I am complying with my request that you show my letter to no one. If I knew that you would let it be seen, all the desire I have for your spiritual progress would not be enough to make me comply.

The account I can give you is: Having found in many books different methods of going to God and diverse practices of the spiritual life, I thought this would serve

Fourteen Letters of Brother Lawrence

rather to puzzle me than facilitate what I sought after, which was nothing but how to become wholly God's. This made me resolve to give the all for the All.

After having given myself wholly to God to make all the satisfaction I could for my sins, I renounced, for the love of Him, everything that was not God; and I began to live as if there was none but He and I in the world.

Sometimes I considered myself before Him as a poor criminal at the feet of his judge. At other times I beheld Him in my heart as my Father, as my God. I worshiped Him as often as I could, keeping my mind in His holy presence and recalling it as often as I found it wandered from Him. I made this my business not only at the appointed times of prayer, but all the time—every hour, every minute, even in the height of my work. I drove from my mind everything that interrupted my thoughts of God.

I found no small pain in this exercise. Yet I continued it, notwithstanding all the difficulties that occurred. I tried not to trouble or disquiet myself when my mind wandered. Such has been my common practice ever since I entered religious life. Though I have done it very imperfectly, I have found great advantages by it. These, I well know, are due to the mercy and goodness of God, because we can do nothing without Him; and I still less than any.

When we are faithful to keep ourselves in His holy presence, and set Him always before us, this hinders our offending Him and doing anything that may displease Him. It also begets in us a holy freedom, and, if I may so speak, a familiarity with God, where, when we ask, He supplies the grace we need. Over time, by often repeating these acts, they become habitual, and the presence of God becomes quite natural to us.

Please give Him thanks with me for His great goodness toward me, which I can never sufficiently express, and for the many favors He has done for so miserable a sinner as I am. May all things praise Him.

Amen.

The Second Letter

To my spiritual advisor:

Not finding my way of life described in books, although it does not bother me, I would appreciate, for my own security, your thoughts about it.

In conversation some days ago, a devout person told me that the spiritual life was a life of grace, which begins with servile fear, is increased by hope of eternal life, and is completed by pure love; that each of these states had its different phases, by which one arrives, at last, at that blessed consummation.

I have not followed these methods. On the contrary, my instincts told me they would discourage me. Instead, at my entrance into religious life, I took a resolution to give myself up to God as the best satisfaction I could make for my sins and, for the love of Him, to renounce all besides.

For the first years, I commonly employed myself during the time set apart for devotion with thoughts of

death, judgment, hell, heaven, and my sins. I continued, for some years, applying my mind carefully the rest
of the day, and even in the midst of my work, to the
presence of God, whom I considered always as with me,
often as in my heart.

At length I began to do the same thing during my set
time of prayer, which gave me joy and consolation. This
practice produced in me so high an esteem for God that
faith alone was enough to assure me.

Such was my beginning. Yet I must tell you that, for
the first ten years, I suffered a great deal. During this time
I fell often and rose again presently. It seemed to me that
all creatures, reason, and God Himself were against me.

The apprehension that I was not devoted to God as I
wished to be, my past sins always on my mind, and the
great unmerited favors that God did for me, were the
source of my suffering and feelings of unworthiness. I
was sometimes troubled with thoughts that to believe
I had received such favors was an effect of my imagination, which pretended to be so soon where others arrived
with great difficulty. At other times I believed it was all a

willful delusion and that there was no hope for me.

Finally, I considered the prospect of spending the rest of my days in these troubles. I discovered that this did not diminish the trust I had in God. In fact, it only served to increase my faith. It then seemed that, all at once, I found myself changed. My soul, which until that time was in trouble, felt a profound inward peace, as if she was in her center and place of rest.

Ever since that time, I walk before God simply, in faith, with humility, and with love. I apply myself diligently to do nothing and think nothing that may displease Him. I hope that when I have done what I can, He will do with me what He pleases.

As for what passes in me at present, I cannot express it. I have no pain or difficulty about my state because I have no will but that of God. I endeavor to accomplish His will in all things. I am so resigned that I would not take up a straw from the ground against His order or from any motive but that of pure love for Him.

I have ceased all forms of devotion and set prayers except those which my state requires. I make it my priority to persevere in His holy presence, wherein I maintain a simple attention and a fond regard for God, which I may call an actual presence of God. Or, to put it another way, it is an ongoing, silent, and private conversation of the soul with God. This gives me much joy and contentment. In short, I am sure, beyond all doubt, that my soul has been with God above these past 30 years. I pass over many things that I may not be tedious to you.

Yet, I think it is appropriate to tell you how I perceive myself before God, whom I behold as my King. I consider myself as the most wretched of men. I am full of faults, flaws, and weaknesses, and have committed all sorts of crimes against his King. In deep regret I confess all my wickedness to Him. I ask His forgiveness. I abandon myself in His hands that He may do what He pleases with me.

My King is full of mercy and goodness. Far from chastising me, He embraces me with love. He makes me eat at His table. He serves me with His own hands and gives me the key to His treasures. He converses and delights Himself with me incessantly, in a thousand and a thousand ways.

And He treats me in all respects as His favorite. In this way I consider myself continually in His holy presence.

My most usual method is this simple attention, an affectionate regard for God to whom I find myself often attached with greater sweetness and delight than that of an infant at the mother's breast. To choose an expression, I would call this state the bosom of God for the inexpressible sweetness that I taste and experience there. If, at any time, my thoughts wander from this state from necessity or infirmity, I am presently recalled by inward emotions so charming and delicious that I cannot find words to describe them.

Please reflect on my considerable sins, of which you are fully informed, rather than on the great favors God does one as unworthy and ungrateful as I am.

As for my set hours of prayer, they are simply a continuation of the same exercise. Sometimes I consider myself as a stone before a carver, whereof He is to make a statue. Presenting myself thus before God, I desire Him to make His perfect image in my soul and render me entirely like Himself.

At other times, when I apply myself to prayer, I feel all my spirit lifted up without any care or effort on my part. This continues as if my soul was suspended yet firmly fixed in God like a center or place of rest.

I know that some charge this state with inactivity, delusion, and self-love. I confess that it is a holy inactivity. And it would be a happy self-love if the soul, in that state, were capable of it. But while the soul is in this repose, she cannot be disturbed by the kinds of things to which she was formerly accustomed. The things that the soul used to depend on would now hinder rather than assist her.

Yet, I cannot see how this could be called delusion, because the soul that enjoys God in this way wants nothing but Him. If this is delusion, then only God can remedy it. Let Him do what He pleases with me. I desire only Him and to be wholly devoted to Him.

Please send me your opinion, as I greatly value and have a singular esteem for your reverence, and am yours.

The Third Letter

For a soldier friend:

Ours is a God who is infinitely gracious and knows all our wants. I always thought that He would reduce you to extremity. He will come in His own time, and when you least expect Him. Hope in Him more than ever. Thank Him with me for the favors He does you, particularly for the courage and patience which He gives you in your afflictions. It is a plain mark of the care He takes of you. Comfort yourself with Him, and give thanks for all.

I admire also the fortitude and bravery of M. God has given him a good disposition and a good will; but he is still a little worldly and somewhat immature. I hope the affliction God has sent him will help him do some reflection and inner searching, and that it may prove to be a wholesome remedy to him. It is a chance for him to put all his trust in God, Who accompanies him everywhere. Let him think of Him as much as he can, especially in time of great danger.

A little lifting up of the heart and a remembrance of God suffices. One act of inward worship, though upon a march with sword in hand, are prayers which, however short, are nevertheless very acceptable to God. And, far from lessening a soldier's courage in occasions of danger, they actually serve to fortify it.

Let him think of God as often as possible. Let him accustom himself, by degrees, to this small but holy exercise. No one sees it, and nothing is easier than to repeat these little adorations all through the day.

Please recommend to him that he think of God the most he can in this way. It is very fit and most necessary for a soldier, who is daily faced with danger to his life, and often to his very salvation.

I hope that God will assist him and all the family, to whom I present my service, being theirs and yours.

The Fourth Letter

To my correspondent:

I am taking this opportunity to tell you about the sentiments of one of our society concerning the admirable effects and continual assistance he receives from the presence of God. May we both profit by them.

(*Editors' note:* Here, perhaps out of modesty, Brother Lawrence switches to the third person to describe his personal experience.)

For the past 40 years his continual care has been to be always with God; and to do nothing, say nothing, and think nothing that may displease Him. He does this without any view or motive except pure love of Him, and because God deserves infinitely more.

He is now so accustomed to that Divine presence that he receives from God continual comfort and peace. For about 30 years, his soul has been filled with joy and delight so continual, and sometimes so great, that he is forced to find ways to hide their appearing outwardly to others who may not understand.

If sometimes he becomes a little distracted from the Divine presence, God gently recalls Himself by a stirring in his soul. This often happens when he is most engaged in his outward chores and tasks. He answers with exact fidelity to these inward drawings, either by an elevation of his heart to God, or by a meek and fond regard for Him, or by such words as love forms on these occasions. For instance, he may say, "My God, here I am all devoted to You," or "Lord, make me according to Your heart."

It seems to him (in fact, he feels it) that this God of love, satisfied with such few words, reposes again and rests in the depth and center of his soul. The experience of these things gives him such certainty that God is always in the innermost part of his soul that he is beyond doubting it under any circumstances.

Judge by this what content and satisfaction he enjoys. While he continually finds within himself so great a treasure, he no longer has any need to search for it. He no longer has any anxiety about finding it, because he now has his treasure open before him and may take what he pleases of it.

He often points out our blindness and exclaims that those who content themselves with so little are to be pitied. God, says he, has infinite treasure to bestow, and we take so little through routine devotion, which lasts but a moment. Blind as we are, we hinder God, and stop the current of His grace. But when He finds a soul penetrated with a lively faith, He pours into it His grace and favors plentifully. There they flow like a torrent, which, after being forcibly stopped against its ordinary course, when it has found a passage, spreads itself with impetuosity and abundance.

Yet we often stop this torrent by the little value we set upon it. Let us stop it no more. Let us enter into ourselves and break down the bank that hinders it. Let us make way for grace. Let us redeem the lost time, for perhaps we have but little left. Death follows us close, so let us be well prepared. We die but once, and a mistake there is irretrievable.

I say again, let us enter into ourselves. The time presses. There is no room for delay. Our souls are at stake. It seems to me that you are prepared and have taken good measures so you will not be taken by surprise. I commend you for it. It is the one thing necessary. We must always work at it, because not to persevere in the spiritual life is to go back. But those who have the gale of the Holy Spirit go forward even in sleep. If the vessel of our soul is still tossed with winds and storms, let us awake the Lord who reposes within. He will quickly calm the sea.

I have taken the liberty to impart to you these good sentiments, that you may compare them with your own. May they serve to rekindle them, if at any time they may be even a little cooled. Let us recall our first favors and remember our early joys and comforts. And, let us benefit from the example and sentiments of this brother who is little known by the world, but known and extremely caressed by God.

I will pray for you. Please pray also for me, as I am yours in our Lord.

The Fifth Letter

To a sister who will soon take her vows:

Today I received two books and a letter from Sister M, who is preparing to make her profession. She desires the prayers of your holy society, and yours in particular. I think she greatly values your support. Please do not disappoint her.

Pray to God that she may take her vows in view of His love alone, with a firm resolution to be wholly devoted to Him. I will send you one of those books about the presence of God; a subject which, in my opinion, contains the whole spiritual life. It seems to me that whoever duly practices it will soon become devout.

I know that for the right practice of it, the heart must be empty of all other things because God will possess the heart alone. As He cannot possess it alone without emptying it of all besides, so, neither can He act there and do in it what He pleases, unless it be left vacant to Him.

There is not in the world a kind of life more sweet

and delightful than that of a continual conversation with God. Only those can comprehend it who practice and experience it. Yet I do not advise that you do it from that motive. It is not pleasure that we ought to seek in this exercise. Let us do it from a principle of love, and because it is God's will for us.

Were I a preacher, I would, above all other things, preach the practice of the presence of God. Were I a director, I would advise all the world to do it, so necessary do I think it, and so easy, too. Ah! Knew we the want we have of the grace and assistance of God, we would never lose sight of Him, no, not for a moment.

Believe me. Immediately make a holy and firm resolution never more to forget Him. Resolve to spend the rest of your days in His sacred presence, deprived of all consolations for the love of Him if He thinks fit. Set heartily about this work, and if you do it sincerely, be assured that you will soon find the effects of it.

I will assist you with my prayers, poor as they are. I recommend myself earnestly to you and those of your holy society.

The Sixth Letter

To a nun:

I have received from M those things you gave her for me. I wonder that you have not given me your thoughts on the little book I sent to you. Set heartily about the practice of it in your old age. It is better late than never.

I cannot imagine how religious persons can live satisfied without the practice of the presence of God. For my part, I keep myself retired with Him in the depth and center of my soul as much as I can. While I am with Him, I fear nothing; but the least turning from Him is insupportable. This practice does not tire the body. It is, however, proper to deprive it sometimes, nay often, of many little pleasures that are innocent and lawful. God will not permit a soul that desires to be devoted entirely to Him to take pleasures other than with Him. That is more than reasonable.

I do not say we must shackle ourselves. No, we must serve God in a holy freedom. We must work faithfully without trouble or disquiet, recalling our mind to God mildly and serenely as often as we find it wandering from Him. It is, however, necessary to put our whole trust in God. We must lay aside all other cares and even some forms of devotion, though very good in themselves, yet such as one often engages in routinely. Those devotions are only means to attain the end.

When we have established a habit of the practice of the presence of God, we are then with Him who is our end. We have no need to return to the means. We may simply continue with Him in our commerce of love, persevering in His holy presence with an act of praise, of adoration, or of desire; or with an act of resignation, or thanksgiving, and in all the ways our spirit can invent.

Be not discouraged by the repugnance that you may find in it from nature. You must sacrifice yourself. At first, one often thinks it a waste of time. But you must go on and resolve to persevere in it until death, notwithstanding all the difficulties that may occur.

I recommend myself to the prayers of your holy society, and yours in particular. I am yours in our Lord.

The Seventh Letter

To a fellow elder: [*Editors' note:* The elder to whom Brother Lawrence writes is, at 64, considerably younger than Brother Lawrence, nearing 80 at the time of this writing]

I pity you a great deal. It will be a great relief if you can leave the care of your affairs to M and spend the remainder of your life only worshiping God. He requires no great matters of us—a little remembrance of Him from time to time, a little adoration. Sometimes to pray for His grace, sometimes to offer Him your sufferings, and sometimes to return Him thanks for the favors He has given you, and still gives you in the midst of your troubles. Console yourself with Him as often as you can. Lift up your heart to Him at your meals and when you are in company. The least little remembrance will always be pleasing to Him.

You need not cry very loud. He is nearer to us than we are aware. We do not always have to be in church to be with God. We may make an oratory of our heart so we can, from time to time, retire to converse with Him in meekness, humility, and love. Everyone is capable of such familiar conversation with God; some more, some less. He knows what we can do.

Let us begin then. Perhaps He expects but one generous resolution on our part. Have courage. We have but little time to live. You are nearly 64, and I am almost 80. Let us live and die with God. Sufferings will be sweet and pleasant while we are with Him. Without Him, the greatest pleasures will be a cruel punishment to us. May He be praised by all.

Gradually become accustomed to worship Him in this way; to beg His grace, to offer Him your heart from time to time; in the midst of your business, even every moment if you can. Do not always scrupulously confine yourself to certain rules or particular forms of devotion. Instead, act in faith with love and humility.

You may assure M of my poor prayers, and that I am their servant, and yours particularly.

The Eighth Letter

To a correspondent:

Concerning wandering thoughts during prayer.

You tell me nothing new. You are not the only one who is troubled with wandering thoughts. Our mind is extremely roving. But the will is mistress of all our faculties. She must recall our stray thoughts and carry them to God as their final end.

If the mind is not sufficiently controlled and disciplined at our first engaging in devotion, it contracts certain bad habits of wandering and dissipation. These are difficult to overcome. The mind can draw us, even against our will, to worldly things. I believe that one remedy for this is to humbly confess our faults and beg God's mercy and help.

I do not advise you to use many words and long discourses in prayer, because they are often the occasions of wandering. Hold yourself in prayer before God, like a dumb or paralytic beggar at a rich man's gate. Let it be your business to keep your mind in the presence of the

Lord. If your mind sometimes wanders and withdraws itself from Him, do not become upset. Trouble and disquiet serve rather to distract the mind than to recollect it. The will must bring it back in tranquility. If you persevere in this manner, God will have pity on you.

One way to recollect the mind easily in the time of prayer, and preserve it more in ease, is not to let it wander too far at other times. Keep your mind strictly in the presence of God. Then, being accustomed to think of Him often, you will find it easy to keep your mind calm in the time of prayer, or at least to recall it from its wanderings. I have told you already of the advantages we may draw from this practice of the presence of God. Let us set about it seriously and pray for one another.

The Ninth Letter

To a nun:

This letter is an answer to that which I received from M. Please deliver it to her. She is full of good will but she would go faster than grace! One does not become holy all at once. I recommend her to your guidance. We ought to help one another by our advice, and yet more by our good example. Please let me hear of her from time to time and whether she is very fervent and obedient.

Let us often consider that our only business in this life is to please God, that perhaps all besides is but folly and vanity. You and I have lived over 40 years in the monastic life. Have we used those years in loving and serving God, who by His mercy has called us to this state and for that very end? I am sometimes filled with shame and confusion when I reflect, on the one hand, on the great favors God has done and continues to do for me; and, on the other, on the ill use I have made of them and my small advancement in the way of perfection.

Since, by His mercy, He gives us yet a little time, let us begin in earnest. Let us repair the lost time. Let us return with full assurance to that Father of mercies, who is always ready to receive us affectionately. Let us generously renounce, for the love of Him, all that is not Himself. He deserves infinitely more. Let us think of Him perpetually. Let us put all our trust in Him.

I have no doubt that we shall soon receive an abundance of His grace, with which we can do all things, and, without which we can do nothing but sin. We cannot escape the dangers that abound in life without the actual and continual help of God. Let us pray to Him for it constantly.

How can we pray to Him without being with Him? How can we be with Him but in thinking of Him often? And how can we often think of Him, but by a holy habit that we should form of it? You will tell me that I always say the same thing. It is true, for this is the best and easiest method I know. I use no other. I advise all the world to do it.

We must know before we can love. In order to know God, we must often think of Him. And when we come to love Him, we shall then also think of Him often, for our heart will be with our treasure.

The Tenth Letter

To my correspondent:

I have had a good deal of difficulty bringing myself to write to M. I do it now purely because you desire me to do so. Please address it and send it to him. It is pleasing to see all the faith you have in God. May He increase it in you more and more. We cannot have too much trust in so good and faithful a Friend who will never fail us in this world or in the next.

If M takes advantage of the loss he has had and puts all his confidence in God, He will soon give him another friend more powerful and more inclined to serve him. He disposes of hearts as He pleases. Perhaps M was too attached to him he has lost. We ought to love our friends, but without encroaching upon the love of God, which must always be first.

Please keep my recommendation in mind that you think of God often; by day, by night, in your business, and even in your diversions. He is always near you and with you. Leave Him not alone. You would think it rude to leave a friend alone who came to visit you. Why, then, must God be neglected? Do not forget Him, but think of Him often. Adore Him continually. Live and die with Him. This is the glorious work of a Christian; in a word, this is our profession. If we do not know it, we must learn it.

I will endeavor to help you with my prayers, and am yours in our Lord.

The Eleventh Letter

To one in great pain:

I do not pray that you may be delivered from your pains, but I pray earnestly that God gives you strength and patience to bear them as long as He pleases. Comfort yourself with Him who holds you fastened to the cross. He will loose you when He thinks fit. Happy are those who suffer with Him. Accustom yourself to suffer in that manner, and seek from Him the strength to endure as much, and as long, as He judges necessary for you.

Worldly people do not comprehend these truths. It is not surprising, though, since they suffer like what they are and not like Christians. They see sickness as a pain against nature and not as a favor from God. Seeing it only in that light, they find nothing in it but grief and distress. But those who consider sickness as coming from the hand of God, out of His mercy, and as the means He uses for their salvation, commonly find sweetness and consolation in it.

I pray that you see that God is often nearer to us and present within us in sickness than in health. Do not rely completely on another physician because God reserves your cure to Himself. Put all your trust in God. You will soon find the effects in your recovery, which we often delay by putting greater faith in medicine than in God. Whatever remedies you use, they will succeed only so far as He permits. When pains come from God, only He can ultimately cure them. He often sends sickness to the body to cure diseases of the soul. Comfort yourself with the Sovereign Physician of both soul and body.

I expect you will say that I am very much at ease, and that I eat and drink at the table of the Lord. You have reason. But think how painful it would be to the greatest criminal in the world to eat at the king's table and be served by him, yet have no assurance of pardon. I believe he would feel an anxiety that nothing could calm except his trust in the goodness of his sovereign. So I assure you, that whatever pleasures I taste at the table of my King, my sins, ever present before my eyes, as well as the uncertainty of my pardon, torment me. Though I accept that torment as something pleasing to God.

Be satisfied with the condition in which God places you. However happy you may think me, I envy you. Pain and suffering would be a paradise to me if I could suffer with my God. The greatest pleasures would be hell if I relished them without Him. My only consolation would be to suffer something for His sake.

I must, in a little time, go to God. What comforts me in this life is that I now see Him by faith. I see Him in such a manner that I sometimes say, I believe no more, but I see. I feel what faith teaches us, and, in that assurance and that practice of faith, I live and die with Him.

Stay with God always. He is the only support and comfort for your affliction. I shall beseech Him to be with you. I present my service.

The Twelfth Letter

To one in great pain:

If we were used to the practice of the presence of God, bodily discomforts would be greatly alleviated. God often permits us to suffer a little to purify our soul and oblige us to stay close to Him.

Have courage. Offer Him your pains, and pray to Him for strength to endure them. Above all, get in the habit of often thinking of God, and forget Him the least you can. Adore Him in your infirmities. Offer yourself to Him from time to time. In the height of your sufferings, humbly and affectionately beseech Him, as a child to his father, to make you conformable to His holy will. I shall endeavor to assist you with my poor prayers.

God has many ways of drawing us to Himself. He sometimes seems to hide Himself from us. But faith alone ought to be our support. Faith is the foundation of our confidence. We must put all our faith in God. He will not fail us in times of need. I do not know how God will dispose of me, but I am always happy. All the world suffers, and I, who deserve the severest discipline, feel joys so continual and great that I can scarcely contain them. I would willingly ask God for a part of your sufferings.

I know my weakness is so great that, if He left me one moment to myself, I would be the most wretched man alive. Yet, I do not know how He could leave me alone because faith gives me as strong a conviction as reason. He never forsakes us until we have first forsaken Him. Let us fear to leave Him. Let us always be with Him. Let us live and die in His presence. Do pray for me, as I pray for you.

The Thirteenth Letter

To one in great pain:

I am sorry to see you suffer so long. What gives me some ease and sweetens the feeling I have about your griefs is that they are proof of God's love for you. See your pains in that view and you will bear them more easily. In your case, it is my opinion that, at this point, you should discontinue human remedies and resign yourself entirely to the providence of God. Perhaps He waits only for that resignation and perfect faith in Him to cure you. Since, in spite of all the care you have taken, treatment has proved unsuccessful and your malady still increases, wait no longer. Put yourself entirely in His hands and expect all from Him.

I told you in my last letter that He sometimes permits bodily discomforts to cure the distempers of the soul. Have courage. Make a virtue of necessity. Do not ask God for deliverance from your pain. Instead, out of love for Him, ask for the strength to resolutely bear all that He pleases, and as long as He pleases. Such prayers are hard at first, but they are very pleasing to God, and become sweet to those who love Him.

Love sweetens pain. When one loves God, one suffers for His sake with joy and courage. I beseech you to do this. Comfort yourself with Him. He is the only Physician for all our illnesses. He is the Father of the afflicted and always ready to help us. He loves us infinitely more than we can imagine. Love Him in return and seek no consolation elsewhere. I hope you will soon receive His comfort.

I will help you with my prayers, poor as they are, and shall always be yours in our Lord.

The Fourteenth Letter

To one in pain:

Thanks to our Lord for having relieved you a little, as you desired. I have often been near death, and I was never so satisfied as then. At those times I did not pray for any relief, but I prayed for strength to suffer with courage, humility, and love. How sweet it is to suffer with God! However great your sufferings may be, receive them with love. It is paradise to suffer and be with Him. If, in this life, we might enjoy the peace of paradise, we must accustom ourselves to a familiar, humble, and affectionate conversation with God.

We must prevent our spirit wandering from Him on all occasions. We must make our heart a spiritual temple so we can constantly adore Him. We must continually watch over ourselves so we do not do anything that may displease Him. When our minds and hearts are filled with God, suffering becomes full of unction and consolation.

I well know that to arrive at this state, the beginning

is very difficult because we must act purely on faith. But, though it is difficult, we know also that we can do all things with the grace of God. He never refuses those who ask earnestly. Knock. Persevere in knocking. I answer for it, that, in His due time, He will open His grace to you. He will grant, all at once, what He has deferred during many years.

Pray to Him for me, as I pray to Him for you. I hope to see Him soon.

Chapter Three

THE FINAL LETTER OF BROTHER LAWRENCE

(*Editors' note:* We chose to place this final letter in its own chapter, due to the singular circumstances in which it was written and the poignant manner in which it summarizes Brother Lawrence's teachings. Written from the monk's deathbed, it glows with a special radiance that bears reading and rereading. We encourage you to pay particular note of the final paragraph of this final letter, in which Brother Lawrence, even in light of his own imminent death, expresses gratitude that his friend's suffering has been lessened.)

To a friend, written from my deathbed:

God knows best what we need. All that He does is for our good. If we knew how much He loves us, we would always be ready to receive both the bitter and the sweet from His hand. It would make no difference. All that came from Him would be pleasing.

The worst afflictions only appear intolerable if we see them in the wrong light. When we see them as coming from the hand of God, and know that it is our loving Father who humbles and distresses us, our sufferings lose their bitterness and can even become a source of consolation.

Let all our efforts go toward knowing God. The more one knows Him, the more one desires to know Him. Knowledge is the measure of love. The deeper and more extensive our knowledge can be, the greater is our love. If our love of God were great, we would love Him equally in pains and pleasures.

We only amuse ourselves by seeking or loving God for any favors that He has or may grant us. Such favors, no matter how great, can never bring us as near to God as can one simple act of faith. Let us seek Him often by faith. He is within us. Seek Him not elsewhere.

We are rude and deserve blame if we leave Him alone to busy ourselves with trifles that do not please Him and perhaps even offend Him. These trifles may one day cost us dearly. Let us begin earnestly to be devoted to Him. Let us cast everything else out of our heart. He wants to possess the heart alone. Beg this favor of Him. If we do all we can, we will soon see that change wrought in us that we so greatly desire.

I cannot thank Him enough for the release from suffering He has given you. I hope for the favor to see Him within a few days. Let us pray for one another.

◇◆◇

(*Editors' note:* Within a few days of writing this letter, Brother Lawrence died peacefully in the monastery in which he had lived his extraordinary life.)

Chapter Four

THE ESSENCE OF *THE CLOUD OF UNKNOWING*

Introduction to the Work

In *The Cloud of Unknowing,* the anonymous author refers to his spiritual path simply as "the work." This path of spiritual growth has a single goal: union with God. The journey takes the seeker through various barriers and layers of illusion until you reach "naked being." In this raw and exalted state, you feel your own nature and the nature of God as one and the same.

The biggest barrier to naked being is the persistent grip of what the author calls Memory. He means something different and much larger than you and I think of as memory. His concept of Memory contains the whole package of pleasurable and painful experiences that we have accumulated in our lives. He also includes in

Memory all of our beliefs about God, ourselves, and the world. All of these must be transcended in order to reach the state of naked being.

When we finally achieve naked being—when the illusions and beliefs and clenches of the past have been released—we are rewarded with a taste of the Infinite. With practice we can go through the world unburdened by Memory of the past and expectation of the future. This is the promise of *The Cloud of Unknowing.*

There are many different versions of *The Cloud of Unknowing,* but none of them is easy to approach. The monk who wrote it was aiming toward the common folk, not for the clergy or the scholars of his time. The original language in which *The Cloud of Unknowing* is written could safely be called a "hard read." In other words, if you want to extract the gold of this work in its original form, prepare to spend quite a bit of time laboring down in the mine. I (Gay) happen to have an enthusiasm for ancient languages, thanks to the inspiration of my boyhood Latin teacher, Miss Emma Williams. Even so, I have a hard time wrestling the 14th-century prose of

The Cloud of Unknowing into plain English. Then, there is the matter of his bluntness. At times he is gentle and loving, but at other times he sounds like a boot-camp drill instructor. Let me show you a key section of the original so you can see what I mean. I'll give you my modern rendition of it first. In this section, the author is telling us how to go about the work:

> *If you think you can comprehend this work with your mind, by using your usual manner of thinking, you are wrong. If you don't stop approaching it this way, and if God doesn't show you the mercy of stopping you, you will fall into frenzies and sentence yourself to complete loss of your body and soul. Be open to God's love as you go about this work. Don't use your cleverness of mind or your imagination, for I tell you truly that these won't work.*

Now, try your hand at finding your way through the original language:

And here may men shortly conceive the manner of this working, and clearly know that It is far from any fantasy, or any false imagination or quaint opinion: the which be brought in, not by such a devout and a meek blind stirring of love, but by a proud, curious, and an imaginative wit. Such a proud, curious wit behoveth always be borne down and stiffly trodden down under foot, if this work shall truly be conceived in purity of spirit. For whoso heareth this work either be read or spoken of, and weeneth that it may, or should, be come to by travail in their wits, and therefore they sit and seek in their wits how that it may be, and in this curiosity they travail their imagination peradventure against the course of nature, and they feign a manner of working the which is neither bodily nor ghostly—truly this man, whatsoever he be, is perilously deceived. Insomuch, that unless God of His great goodness shew His merciful miracle, and make him soon to leave work, and meek him to counsel of proved workers, he shall fall either into frenzies, or else into other great mischiefs of ghostly sins and devils' deceits; through the which he may lightly be lost, both life and soul, without any end. And therefore for God's love be wary in this work, and travail not in thy wits nor in thy imagination on nowise: for I tell thee truly, it may not be come to by travail in them, and therefore leave them and work not with them.

If you think that was hard going, look at his version of another key passage, in which he describes what he means by a "cloud of unknowing":

And ween not, for I call it a darkness or a cloud, that it be any cloud congealed of the humours that flee in the air, nor yet any darkness such as is in thine house on nights when the candle is out. For such a darkness and such a cloud mayest thou imagine with curiosity of wit, for to bear before thine eyes in the lightest day of summer: and also contrariwise in the darkest night of winter, thou mayest imagine a clear shining light. Let be such falsehood. I mean not thus. For when I say darkness, I mean a lacking of knowing:

as all that thing that thou knowest not, or else that thou hast forgotten, it is dark to thee; for thou seest it not with thy ghostly eye. And for this reason it is not called a cloud of the air, but a cloud of unknowing, that is betwixt thee and thy God.

Here's my interpretation of what he's saying here:

When I call it a cloud, I don't mean one made out of moisture, nor do I mean the kind of darkness in your house at night when the candle is out. When I talk about darkness, I mean a lack of knowing. It's a lack of knowing that includes everything you don't know and everything you've forgotten. It's everything you cannot see with your spiritual eye. It is this cloud of unknowing that stands between you and your God.

Remember, he was speaking to the common folk of his time, many of whom were what might be called "metaphorically impaired." That's probably why he was taking care to explain that he wasn't talking about the actual clouds that float around in the sky, or the actual darkness you encountered when you got up in the middle of the night. He was establishing a new metaphor, and a brilliant one at that. He was telling his reader that a veil of illusion, a mental misunderstanding, and a fog of ideas prevented the direct experience of God. He was on his way to communicating the essential message—that love, not mind, was the path, but like all great teachers, he was beginning right where the student was . . . lost in the fog.

The Essence of the Work:
An Experiment in Cloud-Busting

Meteorologists have a slang term for the science of getting clouds to produce rain: cloud-busting. Let's do a little of our own right now, in honor of the earnest monk who wrote *The Cloud of Unknowing*. Let's pause for a moment to do what he asks:

Consciously let go of everything you've been taught and everything you've thought about God, spirituality, and your spiritual path. Just drop it for a moment, much as you might release a sheet of paper from your hand and let it float to the floor. You can always pick it up later.

Now instead of approaching God from your mind, shift your attention to your heart and the love-center of your body. Feel as much love as you possibly can. Love yourself for seeking God. Love God directly. Intend to let love show you the way.

Now, let your mind reengage. You will always have a mind, and thankfully so. Our "clouds of unknowing" often take over, though. There will always be those times when our mind has us in its singular grip, to the exclusion of our heart. Mind and heart can work in union with each other, but the heart is your searchlight for finding God in your life. This is the message that *The Cloud of Unknowing* brings us across the centuries.

Chapter Five

THE CENTERING PRAYER: KEY INTENTIONS AND COMPLETE INSTRUCTIONS

The Centering Prayer is the essence of the teaching offered by the author of *The Cloud of Unknowing*. Remember, the stated goal in *The Cloud of Unknowing* is to remove all the unnecessary "clothing" that obscures our naked being, so that we can feel the actual resonance of God's being with ours. The Centering Prayer is a powerful, simple tool for accomplishing this goal, and it is also a gentle one. This gentleness, combined with its transformational power, makes it an ideal practice for those of us who have been taught that we must suffer in order to grow spiritually. Done according to the instructions, the

Centering Prayer involves no suffering or stress at all; in fact, it feels wonderful.

Now, let's turn to direct, experiential knowledge of this practice.

The Centering Prayer: Intentions and Instructions

Beginning Intentions

Love is the context and background for everything you do in the practice. Open your heart to the power of love, and embrace all your experiences in the spirit of love.

The practice is designed to facilitate you in feeling God's presence in the deepest levels of your being. It is also designed to help you clear away anything that keeps you from feeling the holy presence in every moment of your life.

Begin, then, with these two key intentions:

I consent to feeling God's presence within me at all times.
I consent to embracing all my experiences with love.

Say each of these intentions out loud a few times, then repeat them again quietly to yourself. Try them on, figuratively speaking, as you might don a new jacket or hat. See if they fit for you. If they do, move on to the instructions for the practice.

Complete Instructions

Here are the basic instructions, followed by an explanation of each:

— *The First Instruction: Choosing Your Sacred Word:* Choose a word that represents for you the sacred feeling of God's presence within you. It can be any word that symbolizes your willingness to feel God's presence in you. Here are some that practitioners have found most useful:

Love   Oneness
One   Heart
Union   Soul
I am

You may also use a word of your own creation. Use any word that for you symbolizes the deep experience of God's essence and yours being one and the same. If you do not feel inspired to choose a word at first, engage in a period of prayer in which you invite the Holy Spirit to suggest one for you.

— *The Second Instruction: How to Practice:* Sit comfortably upright. Close your eyes and take 30 seconds to let your system settle down. Then, introduce your sacred word in your mind, as quietly as a faint thought. Repeat your sacred word gently to yourself, letting it find its own rhythm.

It's natural and perfectly all right for your mind to wander from time to time. When you become aware that

you've lost your focus, gently return to repeating your sacred word.

Continue for 15 to 20 minutes. When you reach the end of your prayer period, sit quietly for about two minutes before you open your eyes.

Ideally, engage in this practice twice daily, once in the morning and once in the afternoon or early evening.

Information and Explanations

Once you've chosen a sacred word, use it for the full period of your meditation. To change words in mid-meditation would be to engage in more thinking than the practice is designed to encourage. If you wish to change sacred words, do so before your next practice period.

Do not practice right after meals. The presence of a large amount of food in the body tends to interfere with the practice.

The practice works best when seated upright, spine relatively straight. Do not practice lying down, because for most people, this position is associated with sleep. If, while practicing seated upright, you drift off to sleep, simply treat this as any other train of thought: When you notice that you've been asleep, gently return to your sacred word.

Sit comfortably, but choose furniture that encourages an upright position. You want to be comfortable enough so that you don't find yourself thinking about pain or tension in your body while you are doing the Centering Prayer.

The recommended practice period is 15 to 20 minutes, twice daily. Extending your practice period to 30 or 40 minutes does not improve the Centering Prayer's benefits.

The benefits of practice are best appreciated by its effect on your outer life, not by what experiences you have during your practice sessions. If you go about your daily activities happier and more efficiently, the Centering Prayer is working.

The recommended times for practice are morning (before eating breakfast) and late afternoon/early evening (before eating dinner.) If you want to do the

Centering Prayer after a meal, wait an hour or so until your digestion has done its main work. Don't do your practice at bedtime; it's best thought of as preparation for activity, not as a relaxant or soporific.

It's not necessary to think your sacred word distinctly or clearly, as long as you know you're repeating it. In fact, as you practice you may find that your sacred word becomes so faint that it disappears for a while. This is a normal part of the process; it's actually a good sign that your practice is deepening. In the Middle Ages when the Centering Prayer originated, the instruction was often given to say your sacred word "as gently as you would lay a feather on a piece of cotton."

Thoughts are natural and normal. They're not to be avoided, judged, or criticized. When you're repeating your sacred word, you'll be aware of it one moment, then the next thing you know, you'll realize that you've been off on a chain of thoughts. This is perfectly natural, so no need to judge yourself for it. Whenever you notice you've been off on a thought tangent, simply return to your sacred word.

"Thoughts," in this context, mean the full range of mental events, including memories, fantasies, body sensations, emotion, and commentary. Treat them all as thoughts, and gently return to your sacred word whenever you notice you've lost your concentration.

We hope you enjoyed this book.
If you'd like additional information, please contact:

The Transformational Book Circle
402 W. Ojai Ave.
Ojai, CA 93023
866-288-4469 (customer service)
866-300-4386 (orders)
www.transformationalbookcircle.com
info@transformationalbookcircle.com